THE ON ALL SAID THINGS
MORATORIUM

Marianne Morris

THE ON ALL SAID
THINGS MORATORIUM

ENITHARMON PRESS

First published in 2013
by Enitharmon Press
10 Bury Place
London WC1A 2JL

www.enitharmon.co.uk

Distributed in the UK by
Central Books
99 Wallis Road
London E9 5LN

ISBN: 978-1-907587-62-7

Enitharmon Press gratefully acknowledges the financial support of
Arts Council England through Grants for the Arts.

British Library Cataloguing-in-Publication Data.
A catalogue record for this book is available
from the British Library.

Volume 6 in the Enitharmon New Poets series, dedicated to the memory of
Alan Clodd (1918–2002) and generously funded by his estate.

Designed in Albertina by Libanus Press
and printed in England by SRP

Some of the poems in this book have appeared
in pamphlets published by:
Bad Press, Barque Press, Critical Documents,
Fly By Night Press, Punch Press, Trafficker Press

CONTENTS

Ah the urgency/particularity
of sexual madness as in our man on the street
                                        at the bus
stop catching an eye & pumping up & down his
coat excitedly   so excited
as to forget that the MAIN THING is to get yr
dick out on time i.e.
before the bus blows away. I don't know if he
made it in time I had to look away laughing
because I was on the top deck, out of sight thinking
how I used to think I understood how society works
how no one in their right mind reads *The Telegraph*
but how those thoughts made me so unhappy, &
does a daytime date come over more nonchalant than
a later one, well yes but there's the terrific possibility
you'll spend all day & then the night together as well
forging intimacy where previously there was hard
work   the detached wings of insects attract
me as I stop hoovering & collect what could easily be ignored
ignoring my own, particularly urgent sexual madness
brought up by long evenings. I said to Ruth it's easy
being celibate when no one looks good to you, I said
it to Steve & Jess & Dan & Jamie & my mother as well
                one of those universal truths I guess
                like 'Watergate is not a scandal' it's just the everyday
                creeping & sugaring what would otherwise be
                another dazzling collection of surprises

HIS SILENCE POEM

Just back from the past. It's not even a real place.
I got lost
there to undo
that there ever was a man who knew
better than I how I ought to write
and whether he was dead or alive,
and whether we made
love or not, and whether we were
related or not, it doesn't matter. There is never a war alone.
Now I've been alone. I'd prefer a war. Years and bodies, all mine,
and in every series, one cautiously clapping abdominal set.
Right where I want you. It's true I did once
have my eye on the world. Now I'm the topless recipient of
my own love.

At least I know what I like.

What if all fighting against
is a honing to points
in which things as they are
is in essence release.
The pink rod in my back starts
at the eye in my forehead
I can't close.
It won't be ignored. Stars. They both blink.
Into the bargain I stretch my thighs
taut in tight shorts
and despise proof of my love
as an addiction to blowing and blows.

I mean I'm helpless to a certain sexual power
that is half impotence and half my volition to choose it,
and in thrall to lashing disappointments,

unable to break them, can only stand to cope.
You're a plate. I will break. You get to a point,
you feel sure it's the end, but the curve to an end just perpetuates.
And to others it's freedom, to sleep like this.

Like I said, I'd prefer a war.

Crouching down to compel you in this one,
'I'm calling a spade a spade,' says the pot.
'You're black as a knave,' says the kettle.
In reality, both of them are black
now and both of them used to be white.
Civilians get the gist early on. 'He's a creep.'

On their bellies through thick olive branches they creep
in mysterious allegiance, hair flying into space in this one,
continuing the topical debate of black/white.
'We want reasonable, balanced dialogue,' says the pot.
'It's amazing the way they appease civilians with those black
plush toys, as if admitting greater darkness,' points the kettle.

'There has never been anything more black than that kettle,'
says the pot, bought sweat framing the face, the creep
topless omitted from the. Tank passes in back of a black
and white skirt. White stars liquidized in a black hole in this one.
'Out of my way, you puny little kettle,' says the pot.
They spar over aid-boxes, painted metal tops gleaming white.

'Anyway the dance unit is electrifying,' says a spokesman for the White
Foundation, his face pressed into the ground. Where's the kettle?
The pot sees an opportunity. 'I stand here today as a white pot…'
We don't really know what's going on. The kids creep
harder into their nights of loss. Chairs dashed with glass in this one.
The kettle stares into the mirror, scrubbing at the rings of black.

Brief moment of self-realisation. Will nothing quell the black?
Other than persistent and fraudulent repetition of the word white?
That's not real quelling. A sweaty doll grows his breasts in this one.
'The pot, despite our sanctions, continues with its campaign of black.'

Skulls glitter against velvet pockets as the already-dead creep
breaks humanity's balls. 'You cannot be believed,' says the pot.

'This kettle is completely fucking black,' says the pot,
thinking the microphone is off. YouTube swarms in red and black.
The civilians have long lost interest, deeming each of them a creep.
Meanwhile the avant-garde painters ban the use of white.
The avant-garde poets print books with pages all totally black.
The sun sets on a diseased kind of hope in this one.

Beneath the tomb of public opinion forms the crust of your pie.
Your pie, i.e. a kind of having no allegiance to anything,
whether black, white, this creep or that one, kettle or pot.

It's wholly absurd. Where does the hurt lie, where does the
hurt lie goes the voice, when clearly it lies everywhere,
strewn on the ground under which the city's pipes and drains
have complexity. The water we drink we are not fearful of
dyptheria, malaria, bird flu. We drink, and pour, and brush our teeth
whilst wandering in and out of bathrooms in white vests, each of us
limber, cognitive, pontificating,
maybe gesticulating with the free hand.
I always found this sexy. But it's not like we turn that tap OFF. The boy
wanders through the hallway from the bathroom in a sheer piece of silk.
I impose things upon him,
he is sad, wounded, itching,
tired, depressed, hungry. Inspired, a genius, of prowess.
Those kinds of things start the dialogue off in lovers,
but sometimes dialogue becomes monologue, and there is no way you can
                                                            control
what you say for real, when it counts.
                  Quick, talk to me about finance, quick!
                  Culture is the general sphere of
knowledge, and of representations of lived experience, such as horses,
                                                            within
a historical society divided into economic segments. As though longing
                                                repented her of her
offence. Most unlucky are the properties which they say
belong to lovers. Our lives are no longer entwined. We will
never be together twining
your nerves your mane of
black shining horse and my fingers all entwined,
the hairs like wires going through my body.
                  Most unlucky.
The audio freaked me right out. Then I pretended I was   underwater by
donning a fur headband, then a pair of swim goggles,
then the headphones, the pins popping and unpopping in the
tiny deck chair. My goggles began to fog up. Why? Moisture

being sucked out of my eyeballs of course.

Damn! I shouted as I broke the suction and the orange flooded back, and
Evil was cited in seventeenth-century London's

Bills of Mortality, why not

the 21sts too? Become a historian, why not,

the Bank'll still

take you. You can be James Orr, Ship Finance Manager of
Structured Ship Finance of the Royal Bank of Scotland and I can
be Fra Dolcino. It will

be great. You'll

be great

in bed and

someone will write a song about it. It will be called 'Jism Me
Calm', by the Beat Busters.

Culture issues from

a history that has dissolved the way of life of the old world.

But then someone intervenes and talks about potential

eBay-selling gyps,

like when you refer to something that is only five years old as 'vintage' in
order to get people to buy it. People enjoy being lied to.

But then, as I was saying,

You have not answered the question. It can be like 'Jeopardy!'
Fingers on buzzers. Okay, this *plastic noun* makes artificiality sexual.
Bzz, 'What is silicone breast implant?'
Correct.
You really believed he was following you around.

But then, as I was saying,

the less you see of him hardening inside, the better.

But then, as I was saying,

culture is the only place where the repressed
can seek articulation. That may be a little heavy. Isn't that cool?
She doesn't mind if he sleeps with other people when she's away.
She draws a portrait. It is

the pulchritude of modern man, a shark preying on garbage,
both perverse and earnest, framed by breasts and big rocks. Fuck,
                                        I am literally coming
to be more and more in favour of sweetness,
to love you more and more, Little Rabbit.

ALL I HAVE IS THE BODY TO GO ON WHAT is going on in me. There is movement, always more or less sped up or halted, of consciousness, the movement of consciousness is a vibration in constant flux. Separately to this movement is an aspect of poring over the immediate written past and being unable to divine the written future but trying to, as consciousness takes its new dawn, exactly the essence of its previous but never stopping twice in the same river. The sun hides behind an onslaught of cloud the colour of permanent self-doubt. The absence is one of blaring livefeed and screaming headline, but within that reach of sameness everything is just as it was, and my awareness of myself is not separate to an awareness of others having awareness of themselves, and suddenly the wash of drilling and mining washes over me, the wash of digging and excavating, the permanent wash of greed that washes one way only, and I'm in a room alone in cool air in complete rural silence and everything is impossible insofar as everything is inevitable. I'll stop there.

make it speak, hit it
speech
                      fall to caress lovingly a dead
                      poetry burst its shell & weeps life out
consider the weightless aspect
life in stringy sky & clouds green on faces is a photograph
but a severed also moment I crave
                            anxious made
wait until explosions disperse, as if no one were around well but
there you are, I can't
                    how I mean it is the final surge
                                    but that exactly unends.

ii.

— if that girl, passing, on her mobile phone, is
our mistrusting mistress, time,
and if she looks at me whilst passing
              I am involved in the wild smile —

iii.

sad, slow exercise, poor mechanic,
off on holes with a broken vehicle,
                        tinkering at things
like grief & cold
needs to do this only, it tugs at he
                  blinks back the price in
eyes blood, & dead, & urging now towards the final rest of
sudden silence, unexpected, cannot prevent it now

iv.

oceans of days run out to become other trees,
like music, or water in the bath,
                    forged calm shudders on a daft excuse
& an uncontrollable urge to control
                    & thus remain
glistening on the cusp of an actual shine on it,
            dust polish
                    coping wild to keep that held memory,
                    where you hold
sticks, or finger a vine,
                    disaster of the past, kneading definite memory
                    as something more suitable to this moment
which is cast out,
            vines, cast stomped grape through
            that wringer, your gorgeous split
            throat now opening,
            admitting the sour taste you wait for
constantly, open to suggestion.
            stop, break it. does how it spill then
            mean a thing; when catching up to a point
            in time most wanted for,
                    most caressed & lulled at distance
                    into
being a self desperate wishes. no, stop.
            gathers it in her arms, stooping gathers.
            the poison bush all blossomed & berried
            goes to sit in,
                    picking lyric apart. most
                    natural of exercises,
the sad mechanic picks him up, & a pen,
            forging with sense,
            sense

into a place that rules
it's in your blood now carousing
merry great abundance, grow & get & better &
vitiate, & how
prenuptial, & avoid
disturbing, & it's, &
kill a, enervate, make a
distribution,
without hope is hopeless, that's good,
turn the disaster to a better thing,
though the pain in me lower
than is in me needed,
budding, disproves this theory.
mostly felt in the heart, its own
rhythm collapsing. in a last,
moment, lasting
divided brackets into time.
culling the dainty lyric with a
flick of the disjoint
wrist, admit
collisions & peruse them.
fall to your
look to your
instructed bashes out
eyes & all instruments,
all records of this remove
to what happened
when your world was nothing but its axis
of wild
disturbed words,
all of which cling to nothing, I will say,
how does it go,
in your bed at
morning escaping vicious

words that have racked the skull taunting so
                        long ago as to nearly come
                        mocking up the
                            explains the
this; I see where you are from this protracted
                        filth of action, & I urge
                            you get your
free urge,
           get free of if they are to be that
           sole   hope
                    they must mean what
they must mean all
                that you are
                     my love,
                         I tell you so.

EPITAPH UPON THE VALUE OF HEIRLOOMS

I do not believe in historical darkness
or I do but not weaving itself like lasting hurt
through darkness in the bathroom to find its liberating root in my
impressionable mind or what my grandma did
and felt, hurt drank or any of that I drink
not for an escape into darkness or the genes I parade
they don't care about me and the feeling's mutual. Yes it's clear
that darkest things have happened before. In the room
yesterday after work I got
home and laid
myself among the beanbag. My fall brought up
a cloud of dust I lay watching the sun
and the dust in the light
particles in their own lights until in depthless looking
looked the same as stars or cosmic rays
(whose origins are unknown) and the pleasure
of a poem and the pleasure of looking into space
paralyzed for a long time with a gaggling tongue.
I decide this morning or hear myself thinking
I do not believe in historical darkness. Or I hear
between the bathroom and the past a sinking
option of inevitability but it's optional.

Then back in bed I want
a history of darkness
to make an us inevitable
bursting light through and inaction
and when I think I miss you it's like family.
Acid of wanting always and how
much harder it is now.
Than when I wanted feelings, now
that when I want it's all. Or that
I used to want it all now
only some of it is possible.

CASSETTE TAPE IN ANONYMOUS ENVELOPE

The shadow of physical love is very large
but it fits on my shoulder because
it is so compressed. Compressing a shadow is like
making a black hole, it creates an unbelievable density.
It is why my hips are out of joint. The chiropractor told me so.
If I could find a second shadow things would balance out, there
are good things about certain aspects of balance, but
a second shadow would require a second presence,
and what with the job and the dishes I don't
know if I'm ready to take on
the companion to physical love, which is either
tenderness or a sea of troubles.

But things are good they're good there are good things about
certain aspects of balance. Regarding the glassy pile on the pavement
of aquamarine trinkets
given birth by the burst of youth with its golf-club:
the pop of the windshield is an aspect of balance.
                                    Stop calling me Tom,
the ringing sound is unbearable. It's as if being
underwater and the sounds are the water.
If you swap your tail for a cluster of tin-cans tied to the bumper
then how will you cosy up to the half-dead sailors.
Someone will mock you
                              up, half monkey, half perch
tourists will tickle your hairy belly
until they put you in a glass box and years later a teenager
will point her finger, her mum will cough up and you'll
rot on her bedroom shelf with the sound of Radio 4
congealing in the remains of Sunday lunch.

Now I don't know about you but I jog
carefully I watch where my feet fall.

The other joggers are creating pavement-havoc,
exploding bags of dog shit with their eyeless tread
and hitting the worms with such force that
they actually die. It was the first time I had seen a dead worm.
Normally they keep going. You really have to try
to kill them, but this one was definitely dead I knew because of the blood.
The blood was very red, red as my own.

This is how the sky looks. This is the path for the aeroplane. This is the
new language. This method is
not personal it's just different to yours, ok. Don't worry.
Just look at what I'm omitting.

IS IT OKAY

Writhe in sullen sheets
And under the sheets it's warm
But outside the sheets there's a chill
And but I can't stay entirely under the sheets
And where's the stillness going now
Into the awkward shape of desire
Square head into round hole
Makes the little space tighter
Feet are warm in their blankets
Eyes lidded like nighttime how
Will I break into this day from
Here alcohol and my self coercion
The electricity brings good
Things and some bad
Things to get caught up in the prime
Minister to say I can't sleep
With him why does he
Pummel our country to punish
Back to the blankets I never left
Back to the heavy lids and residues
Of stanching my self coercion
Music trilling the tree
Air so grey so turbid mess
Breathe into the heart I know
It's there among the tightness and bubbles
Among the fucking and waxing
Among the distance and separation
Among the sending well wishes even
Though I hate her
Bubbles move down
Saying yes it's okay
It's okay to

Come on
A Tory
A frenzy
To be convinced of anything
Of you can trust

There is no woman here to speak, to say "Mind the nails for the dress,
not to rip, at the hem, off a piece." Instead there is one to say "the
dress had been given me along with the makeup it is a woman's
requirement that she be unwilling. Put these and this on they
said and you'll do it because of the passport."
      The knave of cups sits at the side of the bed in lemon yellow.
Freud leaps about in the wings wearing a red
chicken-print leotard. The real battles are staged
now down dotted grey lines of territory that finger the buildings
nefariously, delineating anaesthetised fucking
and personal space.

      On the table-track of streets, cracked lines find
fault with the person that pushes past. I have love in me. That's not how
I fuck. I heard a lot of the sports guys saying that it was fun sometimes
to take a woman down a peg or two – because she knew she was hot –
by fucking her. But she liked it that
way, it meant she was right in her thinking. She
has a pile of trophies in her duvet cover.

      Is this who you are?
      Is this what you do?

      In disgust I found a well of love, its little care
marked by contrast. Looking through the smeared glass I came
upon rows upon rows of autocolours, all of them tangential greys.
"From within this spectrum we are permitted to access God."

The fishing has been good this week. In the flat. There
have been a lot of fish. The best thing was that I didn't have to
actually fish for them, it was more a case of
snatch and grab. There was clean death enacted, I read about it
on the train as it lulled and pumped the track til my district.
The deaths were announced on the front page – fish death

in M.M.'s district. I heard about it through a friend. I was innocent
but there was a paper trail from the door of my job to the door
of my home, of receipts and tickets, indicating my penchants.
But seeing as how it was just a few fish, all I needed
do was press conference and subsequent release:
M.M. in shame shock. Coleen. Ethical consumption. Things of real substance
put yourself into a gill ticket. This can be done by cutting a ticket into strips
stapling the strips with fish skin
fan the strips place them in arrangements
around your body as it bends thoughtlessly
over the broken bed. Ramos de jacintos.

In the romp and dust of my hands I find the remains of birds.
I stare down at my hands in disbelief. Have I done it again, I wonder.

That night, and on the following nights and like the previous nights
I sleep in a strange bed. The price for a bed
now is a body. Reproduction is practically
an accident.

MEAT BEACH

Today is average but totally unique
I decide I am not going to blame myself
even though travel is clearly becoming a
series of attempts at psychological avoidance
                        & go instead artificially
winged. Leap from minimal heights, avoid
butterfly knives, apply drool to the skin
over bone, under toes the jellyfish are clear
dice with no spots, find myself walking on
constructs of rust feet and feet up,
poisonous weeds and jetsam beneath
walking the fine beam
I wonder
whether or not I can get across this block
of butterflied meat in my mind, which moves
with money,
like an eloquent philosopher/
butcher/dog, who
despite bloody face and hands
speaks well on the subject of life.
Self love, self denial, and self sufficiency
get the lonely point across.

All day I fly a drunken kite on the beach
                energy is the   blues bright
hello I can't muster, sorry
                for the sadness
in my eyes when I can't say goodbye,
                preoccupied by travel
and its   psychological avoidance.
                The old rule of
no matter where you go, there you are.

POOR ELEPHANTS POEM

You are a poor elephant who aped me
and I am a poor elephant who aped you
and it wasn't even a real elephant to begin with
and I don't know why we're friends.
There I said it.
Here I am brilliantly foreclosing all of the deals
but actually doing the opposite of all that
under the general bracket of 'life's work'
patiently detecting the humus in which
I have been secreted, shiny except from having been
polished with piss instead of whatever
it is that they use to polish trains. I can't even
talk about what the ocean's been doing today,
mimicking an orchestra and the nightclub
happenings of youth, script that won't play,
smiling clouds, absent mermaids inferred through
erumpent achievements of explosive hydrous.
An acorn, a chestnut. Can't help repeating
the things that were said to you in moments
of youth, even as you say them to yourself.
Say them to yourself thinking that all is
understood, that every unconscious
thing said is a thing said
to the sayer in memory so deep and convoluted
it's like birth
remember they invented logic
but how can you, as a listener,
discern between conscious and unconscious
utterance, particularly when neither of those
two things really probably exist anymore.
These informative images do not evoke my
situation, who do they hope to entice?
What do they hope to effect? Hope is
encouraging but when invisible and absent

and no one can find her as she went out just
for a run but ended up at the bottom of the
river, which flooded the highway this after
noon bringing death to our door, it's
hard to see anything but the end.
If I wanted to give myself or this poem
some abstract epithet like 'Beast of Bernini'
I would have to
prove to you
slowly, over
several minutes
and repetitions, how I
am both the fingering structure that
reaches after eternity and
made of white marble, which cannot be pierced,
only caressed from the outside hard panel,
how I am not simply hardened, or softened,
a dance of opposites or forgetfulness,
how I am helpless as the next when
hoping to achieve comfort.
If I wanted to call myself any kind of name at all I would have to
not just paint a picture of two women dancing,
one the width of a wrist, the other
nicely filling out a pair of overalls.
I won't call myself anything,
my feet are too light
driving off
into reality which location I can't
ever seem to get to,
and all of that seems insurmountable now and
I don't trust you, etc. I now regret which
things have brought me to the
headline, 'Why
England Retained the Ashes', nestling alongside

death squads and terror plots and the Vatican.
But luckily the news
is entwined with compatible accomplices
who prefer being in the spotlight to
reading about somebody badly screwing
some other body.
Mounds of leftover feasts fester in vitriol,
clothes fresh from the factory,
for some reason the inclusion of me in its audience
and I'm supposed to a) lap this up b) feel bad about it c)
apologise and d) refrain increasingly from my own
life as if something bigger than us really were—
is there any point to this it's so messy I'm so sorry.

A pinprick. Languages
sing in their dictionaries, the covers shut, considering the
soft fervour moments take on once they have passed
and it is safe to rewrite them. One says, on reflection,
that was such and such a moment, and perhaps another
will agree. But at the time no such thing existed
and in this way we are all authors. Generalities
and the uniqueness of certain things.
It's silence that gives birth to them and
then swallows them up, the entire mystery
congealing in someone's mind a vast
internal dialogue of birth and silence and death
can span any number of weeks, its longevity
coming to mean nothing if death is a certainty and it is.
As you are born, so you shall go: under pressure,
wrought in the privacy of how thought wanders
inventing the connecting wires, what shall we
talk about next. Viciously sweet moments ensue
passing between real eyes. Thought wanders again,
leaves the present company to reminisce about the
not-too-determined future and presses into its hands
the petals of a dying rose. Scentless pieces. The
thought returning each time to a
site of sadness that glimmers with the
compromise of return. Then all the other possible
compromises become
laughable by turns having been silently exhausted having
never been tried. Measure out the cups of flour
press them to her neck turning her face away,
the shoes stuck on.

MAGDALENE

I'm sitting in the middle ground, the building's boundless peace
confounded by its domes deflecting heat and eating sound –
they eat the sound of silent crying, observe the head
submerged in fingers cupping griefs of mishap.
I wonder will the balance continue to increase,
and stretch my ears out longing to be cupped by sound,
which is being eaten by the ceiling.

An inundation not completed metes its dolor out in decibels
all whispered. The story is forgiving, and my heart,
in little lines, a metered search for calibration. I'm going
                                    to reenact this later
as a ragged scream expressing bestial loss. Words are present, everything.
Face is wrapped in fingers teaching secrets to their blood and
keeping all of them from me, the head revolting.

These conversations have been useful, but it pains me to admit them,
their suggested lactic souring, at every edge walks beauty's danger,
cracks the mirror, letting flow the run of watery blood
congealing, but in the fervent moment of its letting
still seems less of life than all internal crises.

Doctor, put your hands upon me. Hold my head between your two palms
warm with blood contained correctly. Love at distance, parachuting,
holds through gales, renewed by danger. All the same, did not the mishaps
clustered in these vaults of heaven hold me close, admitting ruin? There is nothing
I won't lose. In confirmation, a foreign voice butchers the average day. I turn,
her skirt is hitched up like a Viking. Her pale, decrepit flesh is slackened.
                              Purify the stream that flows, ammonia from
my mouth I do not know whom I'm entreating. Why suddenly so damned,
when at my back there is, retreating, a flow of grace that was unbounded,
daily counted, daily reaped by the same fingers that now clutch

my eyes behind their visor. Each of my hands the other holding, rubbing,
stroking, hope the blood will stir to solely inward motion.

By the way, I have
a set of postcards. Most depicting naked women, but some are technical
appropriations of a very famous building. I find a woman's body
very like a famous building.

LULLABY NEVER WORK

Downstairs the little voice cries in anguish
at having been born recently, enough
to anguish anyone, anguish
dulled in the safety of
passing years, sleeps
repressed and is occasionally
        articulated in the vapor of dreams.
The thing that makes you smoke when you are
already coughing up blood, the rare dream of satis
leading to inevitable immolation on the pyre, good
bye husband and with you myself, you were all that I am.

Vexing games played against conscious will, one:
                The Defence
Secretary eats the fish eyes and the eyes breed in the
Defence Secretary's belly and then pop out of the De-
fence Secretary's skin, a thousandfish-sight breaking the
demonstration staged by the Defence Secretary's flesh.
            All of the eyes blink in unison, you
can hear the gulp of the wetted epidermis.

           Vexing games [. . .], two:
The seating arrangement was "done" by
the butterfly swarming on her face as it ate
serotonin from a doggy bag of past envy.
Then the weird fact of pets being owned and their
polystyrene beds and the shit of the world fairly ablaze,
the usefulness of latex, rubberized veins, and lithium,
then you lick salt off the blancmange. Dying Alone
runs down your leg, as the voices of men cook
in oil against your chest where the hurt is caked,
clasping the unconscious minnow.

Dying Alone curls itself round your thigh. To
finally fuck standing up, that will be the death of me. I hope
you feel the same way too, then we can get the cheapest
ironing-board and lip-synch in the aisle to something awful
as our double-paean to death is formulated in the privacy
of our shared thoughts, milk in our
mouths like the good old days. This
is a choice, but it's not exactly your
fault. Just go to work, it's easier that way. The droll
insufficiency of wages pings like static in a pyjama top.

A LUMBERING OBVIOUS BEAR CALLED
WHOYOUHANGOUTWITH

Is there a line between care and apathy
and is it boy-shaped as I haven't decided on a mortgage location
is it boy-shaped as I haven't decided about clubbing
boy-shaped as the car is driven down and to the right
am I an arty barrage if I fit in this social adhesion
this particular coercion here of class bracket and then decision
the money that I impose symbolically on how I believe
and to how I believe raise
a several glass. Not angry that images take over
advance accidental hugs and brunch
reconciling to the bathroom for some minutes
home to watch beauty dryly drilled in its pucker
and the trouble to care about the stream of conjecture
that touches on money but not how to have it
solids go runny
people give themselves out
I am in a horde on a street
having given myself out
of the building in time
to leave with the lights and prowl about looking for food
I can't raise this one
to the conclusion it wants necessary
only say that I can't escape certain things and that certain things
are a trap for a lumbering obvious bear called WhoYouHangOutWith

ALL I HAVE IS THE BODY TO GO ON

The feeling of knowing always comes first through the guts, a cooling and loosening how organs know and how I know and how I am my organs knowing and warming and then cooling, churning and then knowing and then cooling and then churning. The information is feeling, always either more and less or more fully or less fully itself, until I have to go make soup of myself through the pen and I hold water in and hold other liquids in. And then the girls break their silences in their dresses all anticipating the lifting of their layers, and I am suspiciously clothed in the rigorous silence in which petticoats and hair are interchangeable with the churning of my organs, and I arrive in a snowstorm, I am going to be hail and hailed, the robes are going to fall and be gathered and then fall again, and my arm will be cool and then warm again, and all of the men around me will be abundantly hairy and rhythmic, bent over their technology as it thieves from them the value of their labour, thieves from them their corporeal values, and through the mincer in corporeal passings our bodies slink beneath the cracked sill like oil.

The landscape
is black with forced clarity
to grow up
  master intricacies
    language doesn't fit
    easily with
thought .poetry
is, *the bed brackets the mind*

in insomniacs

Golden Globes 2010 WORST-Dressed: See Who Committed
what you asked for was given
moral judgment on the hay-coloured truss not omitted,
don't cleave, it shouted openly, split off into various
documenting is a public process
    the repetition of the image
see who committed
gaze under electric light
    too long at any one thing
    the repetition of the image
      see who committed
    care enough to want to know

what do you call a man with no shins
what do you call a man
what do you call a group of pigs
what do you call people from hong kong
what do you call a
what do you call a baby rabbit
what do you call a pregnant fish
    and disappointment disappeared

instantly Wikipedia'd by force through
        catastrophic magnitude 7.0 M_w.
Here you are and I've named you,
        naming made you cheap.
What is it you're not saying

Is my school closed
Is my car insured
Is my car taxed
Is my dog pregnant
Is my tv hd ready
Is my cat pregnant
Is my train on time
Is my school open
Is my house haunted

      I won't tell you his name
      nor mention any flippant cry
absorb fantasy.
It is political to name names,
            they say.
        EARLY on Monday January 17th, just as x were settling
to work, the heart of X came under attack from a well-
organised x of x, many rigged up as x. They x at x, a x, a x
and a hotel frequented by x. But by mid-afternoon the x
had either x or been killed by local x. The violence left at
least x dead (including several x) and x injured; it also
reinforced a growing sense of vulnerability in the capital
stays replete with lasting feeling.
Amortize until rigor mortis
advertise rigorous immoral but moreover
the tactic is one of subtlety.
           Directly trace this into work,
      how I believed it was contrived but did not know how

could not vent offense on the air much as I'd like
        to be a good person,
        the goat must shine on you.
It is so politic to leave names lying around
        ornamenting your beetle
        tattooing your butt
        curtains in ancient drag
        froth of digital harm
        buried underneath cardboard and styrofoam
        layers of implied filth
    this image that has no time
    this image that has no place
        that situates us in encyclopedic moments
        like a shadow who raged so
    it made us afraid
    I had better not know
what I'm saying, lest some European death take hold, and crow glory
    like a vulturous semen doll,
        stained with earth in the hose
I sowed with grass seed to soften.
        If you write
        in the shadow
        of the image you had better write quick
        & maybe — can hear yourself thinking
                sighs at Seneca
                yawns at Aristotle

TOO MUCH IN THE SUN

what is a means to access a force of good
to seek be a strive for a
force to good meaning
nothing you can try
with conviction anyway
failing in whomsoever's
beard falling
deep into whomsoever's
beard

Maybe time to let the good guys
to the front of the queue at newsstands
get them faster the news
of screen-warring peroxide
adopters of fetishised
Live 8 poverty
while the poverty we have
not directly sanctioned
     with pop music
         and costly herd
goes bang all day long

as holiday planes avoid the airspace
as you would in your dress
sucking the air around
a wraith-like erection tagged
complaisance. Yes you in need of
news of warring

peroxide adopters of
fetishised poverty permanently
elated on the edge
of new plastic
developments in word or in
deed we are the blind spot
from whence all of vision
curves, beauty: it curves, curves
are beauty, whispered words
interviewed by makeuppy foaming
features what else you think about unthinkable
things happening on your street.

Terrorised by slickers
of gloss that plump the linoleum
nest around our indelible
shoes and face with their value added
    emptiness, postering the air behind the
bounce of the gravid
womb round the autobus craters.

THE AUCTION

Nobody starts out wanting an auction but you make them come
round, but there's little inevitability there, no guarantee
that sleeping lovers wake
to love.
                       A disturbing hint of milk and
our carnivorous stage manager is shouting about the auction
                                     we are having,

          the one no one wants.
As he descends he becomes authoritatively beautiful all right.
A woman appeased by pink bids exuberantly for a submission
          of which she is unaware. This is a wager
on certain events whose significance deflates in
aristocratic lunch parties but which recovers when
                    during the costumed drinks

a heap of bodies piles up and someone has to be taken
into confidence. Once, you were young and unbroken,
possessed of a submission that had not yet been allocated.

A man's body descends for a seat, his cool hands certain
of wanting and temporary light. What brews is an
emaciated lust you buy back with the fire of your bid.
Try to blame the cold sweat on your last real lover,
recall doing each other in speech. The bid swarms
accidentally where you fanned your face. How much
do you want it. Take me to the shop. Now I get on
the train. Now I wait for you for dinner again.

The stage manager glistens at the forefront, recalling
KY. You can say anything, your bid can say any
thing and your emails can say anything, but you
yourself sit in back of the kitchen. Now banish

wishes from language, they take up space, and time.
I will never be where you think you find me, and if I were
to find myself as skin growing hard over a wound of no
origin you would be the last to know. Everyone wants to
use an author as a mirror but the hottest temperatures
generate in complicity.

You did not really want to bid, only witness it going down,
this little lie, the memory of perverse pleasure buried in
an embrace that takes breath away. Eventually it will bust out,
like pressurized cream among fingers.
The bidder has not nearly enough to throw away,
and the text that will never be framed rests living in the soul
of whoever cannot let it go.

2 ANGELS

1 a)

scoping
        wildly the brimming curve, toss-eyed,
angel's
        nerves beat the plastic
kiss
        of the clouds whilst waiting
somnambulant drizzle
the paper paste on
        and expect it to stick, this
kind of love   bastes slow juice over and kick
it
        backs up the mix of a
beautiful
        face

or b)

no sharp
        undulled in the windbroken rains,
hard,
        sharps, dulls, sharps, every semester a
coal grey lampshade
knocked off the side of your head.
        the colours leak out to phosphorous
pools
        of patented rainbows, and rainclouds, this

kind of love   gnarl at the end of the garden
refusing to alter the clip of it, wild to suffer,
cross and divide will always take more lines

2)

rubbish night decides sweeping the shock in, swirl
a bone clasped to the chest, bat your tongue no
                more must collect the overawed
                actual bliss keeps distance so
as not to be just; blasted pulses bleeding milk
soft out casings and the speed of love; spurted
                over-fresh a day, some days,
                the railings click uncountable
by; shy away from love and its grateful speed
                which is too great or lasting in speed
nasty flower on her, changes languor to speed
                terrific possibilities such as her speed

what you think alters satisfactory as sugar
moods burn and you sense it. could nothing
break simpler or smooth itself over beaches
or drip straight from the bottle i love you

sort of
morning. Then I watch today crossing the bridge
by the eye & large houses for evidence
of the specimen I've come to acquaintance with:
a life shutting out realities, cloy of loud music
thumbing the brain, an unwillingness
to look at the fellow pedestrians in their
face wind-bloated & wearied eyes, hair white
the scowl of Marks & Spencer flowers flogging blooming
across the windows in GB
pounds gaudiness slumped
with the lie, milk & walk for the day is
coloured by insufficiencies borne on my
heart London I live in you with distance
topping over the bridge-line people in
black resemble crows, feet resembling cyclists the smear
on glass & learn to edge off expectation, I dying have 666
Boots Advantage points & my bones

                         tersely into the
                         a stress grip too

loving the notion of a demise now press &
release. The ache of a self-spoken heart does
exactly what it's told, inchoate references connect by
bleeding out a milky casing remnant. Is there another
way this can work all day at data entry &
never gets tired it has a name its name is
Carla XP5000, her brain is sounder than yours
because she didn't have to fight the GCSE it's all
in the chip & polish, potentially you now
have the opportunity to get on with more
important things like the administration of

your own life into boxes says the voice of
the fat controller, his cheeks
creak with the spank of cash But I want my
paycheque I creak diminishing songs &
rules choking on the kidney bean salad. All
I am & shifting data left right painstaking
loss of imagery at every sight, step. The tourists drop their
jaws, point their devices at the Eye & large Houses,
representation has already told them
once they see it for real before them in their
three biological dimensions they will without
a doubt be in London. That's all a city is now
proof of recognition via simulation & retelling.
Some people are running out of the church with smiles on
church conversion to arts & crafts fair stems
come out the tops of tomatoes think of

> that think of that
> pus like lemon under
> skin, gibbering hair

Pollution knows a boundless image,
creeping about the pressed paper or stop & I'm
crying one night, she said through hair, pieces stuffed
in & against her mouth wet with pain, spit
or pleasure, pain's great bitch. Rub antonyms
into saggy, broken skin is what the mirror image
looked like in part when bathroom black eyed
salt-lick mirroring hating my eyes & ours
     sort of
      morning
      ennui threats with its laze & gauze bodies
      stretched arched on blue cotton
         taut on blue
         caught on

mildewed by lateness I lack a noun
against my legs whitened coming winter.
      His turning face
        the kitchen taps
          the winning mark

              he has the standard exit wound.
              Start up & break it again with
              not much damage done, pray for damage
              to come again. Or shouts violent bladder
              ring-fish-pull.

              Speed sleeps at his teeth like a river fish, the
              thud more & more of death, words
              just coming freaking
              out the boy looked

              I wanted to run
              perish on

this drab buck for love runny in turpitude &
elision, having the time to fight. Do I
drop bliss-marks down around my ankles, leave
out the qualifying agent or a clawed back bank
of skin, here is the recharger, edit with epithets
scar fades to a loose nipple from which used to
be a heart. Lie under with love for the home,
always absent, always dripping from it upturn
all this tooth & nail-varnish drabber stanch
blood flowing from the kitchen taps hot &
cold again, eyes in twenty four hours contain
all of life, enough to make you say all of life.

The things you threw away.
    The things you lost.
        Never gave yourself again fully,
ever, really. Never thrashed
    with a full heart.
Never lay in the dirt elated.
    Among garbage, on wooden boards.
      On counter tops, against water jugs,
        on mushrooms, on cake.
THE ICING ON CAKE.
    You find the kitchen ordinary
      until suddenly

A FUCKING ANGEL DESCENDS!
OUT OF THE FACE OF A LIVING   !
MAN AND SAYS, BEHOLD MY
COMING, I AM LOSING THE
CONNECTION WAIT HOLD ON...
BEHOLD MY COMING, A MYSTICAL –
I AM NOT OF THEE OR THINE NO
WAIT ... NO IT'S GONE ... I'VE LOST IT

Amongst the angels that season frog-tying was the cool thing to
do and they would exchange. Frog ties which were long green
strips made from dead frogs, the skin cured and moulded until
supple.
              They were expensive because everyone wanted one.
They were inexpensive because everyone had one.
They were inexpensive because everyone wanted one.
They were expensive because everyone had one.

The trouble was, you inattentive lovers, one of victory.
A template of blown wind through the mouth of a cloud,
blushing into the mirror that curves up like beef powder
as impacted and hard-hitting as the journalist's
checkpoint, it shoots first and says 'do you
have ID' afterwards, in English,
and the journalist is
coming.

Fish have more trust in them*selves*.

Your friend Jimmy Blair would be a more sensible choice would be
       hard-pressed to
say, in public, perhaps over some mince pies and mulled wine, that he
doesn't give a shit about injustice on a world scale (leaping forms of
       angels, their ankles

                frog-tied

their aprons lactating); but it would be
easy for Jimmy Blair to say that he thinks the poem is a cunt. There is no
       quotient of lust.
No one else needs to know where it is that you feel that particular pain.

HUM POEM

In the space that was singing I shut myself
up in the spinal space of leather
curving into me   drifting off   humble estate
of my humanity to hum verse

to sing powerless lines
quietly at a hum from inside the house
as the sun breaks out-
side over irrational sleep and between the
electrical lines my mind dawns down my hum-
anity any of me making a hum-
an offering reaching out sleepily

where is the moon
and where is the sun where are
the sunken fields

I do not know how to make a poetic thought.
I do not know how to make a poetic thought
instead of envisioned. See dahlias and birch trees,
want to say 'fighter pilot' and 'ribbon'.
Confuse inspiration with alchemy,
politics with promiscuity,
small comforts with abuse, what's the use
of poetry, Keston, I ask, to think yourself
into language that makes you live your life differently,
he says, everything I want I have, I think, but
you're a man and I'm a woman, I say,
maybe things are different for men and women.
Maybe, he says. Some things are the same, though.
Like peeing, I say.
Yes, he says, like peeing.
The trees stretch their tendrils into blue heaven.
The birch is a forgotten prize. I am too high up to
really get at the dahlias.

Johny drove over a toad yesterday. 'It really upset me.'
Did it explode, I wonder aloud. Was it a big one?
Did you stop the car?
No, he says. He smiles.
I can't see very well
through the dark
the faces of others
but I know a cold
sore occupies half of mine.
Morality is the health
grid along which my
body is organised and I
have been 'very bad'.
Can I say I'm

oppressed by the male gaze.
Is that what happens when you have
the body of a stout gazelle and love Pasolini
can identify that structures
of academic thought reproduce
but can't say why, have had school
paid to feed you with a hot, gummy spoon?
That spoon I spat out as if it was metal and slumped in the chair.
Others swallowed the spoon, are lawyers. Others
are married with the spoon comfy there, pancreatic.
For our honeymoon we went to the islets of Langerhans.

Every hawker of reason
from Anselm of Canterbury to Jacques Rancière
makes language her trampoline into the sublime
with the leaping that gets her high
enough viewed alternatively as
a suffocating discourse on art
a regime for identifying art
the condemnation of Pelagianism
the constitution of an indistinct sphere
vicious circles in arguments
the endless work of mourning
the Word of God
the right, the true,
the aesthetic utopia, the totalitarian utopia,
all utopias after all is said and done you're helpless and sleeping
aliquid quo maius cogitari non potest

to arrive always at the same ineffable wall
the route inwards increasingly convoluted
centuries, technology. Seek knowledge through constant
duality of self and other always
the same vulnerable mess confirmed you as a friend.

I pick up my the *Collected*
Poems of Frank O'Hara,
not even to read, just to be close
and sun sings through the curtain
willing all negation to dance itself
to a club I can't get into and leave
me alone to my meadow
and inverse twin bedded
down there where what I imagine
making on wheat-coloured grass
is not tapered and short, is not
a bent staple in my sacrum thinking
that way is a direct line to the fridge,
but the perfect my other whoever I like.

The safety of returning to the same old rhyme:
princess in tower is happily after
forever—were men damaged by this?
Or was it just the girls, the failure of this
hope then, a specific logic of the real
is pride in how I drive her (the car),
an image of impoverished feminism,
necessarily just to the adult male citizens.

You say you are trying to make the everyday
vibrant with being not
cleaving to pulsion and in so
doing seek in every
permission a man.
Hegel said it best when he said
[a]ction by one side only would be useless because what is to happen can
only be brought about by both[,]
the mirror has been establishing itself all this time,

and yet all I can see in it are my errors.
This means we are looking into mirrors of errors.
This means we require each other's tenderness.
The wind is furious, the winter coming hard.
Did it feel like the end of your relationship, she asks.
It's hard when winter comes on, she says.
I pushed myself too hard, I say. The answers
Wear masks.

ON THE THIRD DAY JOE ROSE AGAIN

The light ever-changing proof changeling. Walk
       into ownership willing fist open locks
(begging) shut them fast oh
       depth proffered, never more alive
than on the edge of collapse
       from the remembered state into the union-
idealised state, we are addicted to something
       all right, just look at the oppression of beef.

       Intelligence we trouble to understand
gazes back photographed in us.
       In years to come these photographs
will shock us more than severed limbs,
       for severed limbs are compulsions
fabrics of ourselves.
                        It will be meat
                        that comes to stare us down.

The impropriety of
       continuing to shock at tea and your inner self was a house divided
against itself and the expensive infringements
       of politics. Shock and awe
even whilst the ordinary quality
       of beauty in you goes unnoticed
excessive caution has bred imbalance
       by all you claim to know. Against a light internalised
from the switches, parade of you. And
       plugs. Now and then you meet an adversary & all you can do is fight
them, mostly
       in bed

       halve them
slice you open draw chalky lines of limits

over polarised landscapes
and step across. At the desk flesh considers
		the organs of your loved one, for whom psychology is a distant
longing, teasing breath. Does love ache so, so
		make itself unavoidable, whilst the heart
is a play about a church under fire. Templar dot.
		The naked enemies plant seeds
of death and sedition which is
		merely a mode of truth, of good intent
or an instance of being
		locked into addiction.

HYPOTHETICAL REPRESENTATION

the wasteful
origami
billionaires,
their hypothetical
diggings
of landfills
an arrow sticking in a bin
upturned into the mealy owned earth
and the real hole in the real earth
clucked by chicken wire
as opposed
to a rinse over the
marks between the
lanes of the
traffic in the rain
the traffic in the rain
the traffic in the rain
the repeatable traffic in the repeatable rain

"I will not
look at myself and I will not
seek to look at myself"
who would ever say that
someone who cares
about that waste

MURDOCH CAN'T BUY ME LOVE

To swoop with your vision is the limit of the
elision of your dreams at the hands of Mind Corp., a
stupid white male who can't pick his own dreams,
needs phenylalanine to deal with the paper coated in the arm of
his own arm, his own hedge fund arm, his corporate broking arm.
When I change my MySpace picture to a picture of his
face and win the Face of the Week Award, handsome, Screw
Corp.,

    a no-

           thing, no more things can be plucked from the air
           now you read it to feel it politically Handsome
           Nationalist Racist Muscly Arms Corp,
           pie in the face, thing you make in you come
           up and bounce off the taped mirror
           devouring itself on playback, agreeing
           beforehand on £15 with tip, and after
           Khalif's biography about the kids back home and
           the dust the fallen truck kicks up, crying
           successfully, ethically wasted, financially rinsed.
           How now do you feel about repetition because
           some of them beep a hundred times in the same arrangement
    and no
one insists on talking about it in parliament let alone pointing it out.
Put the lab rabbit in therapy. I just hate how everything
makes sense, the Pope wearing ermine, loving all
god's creatures, except the girls, the boys, the ermine, the gays.
The Vatican, the Europa Multiclub. It's foolish
to imagine there is a destination not too equipped with fire
for those whose heads yap their scintillating hypocrisies
when I am ashamed of merely having been sucking waffles
drenched in the news of News Corp's desires and
praising the energetic necessity of love at the same time,
fouling the air of a merely hypothetical intimacy, AND

love is the thing that I need, broadly speaking, though
it can easily be affixed, broadly speaking, for example to
the fronts of things, to their lexical surfaces, in a
taupe ballerina dress worn by the anorexic that
      the guys say is hot that
        the girls say is anorexic that
        the designer wants for the runway that
        the South American fucks winningly
        let's not go into it
        suffice to say it can be easily affixed.
        Bloody spray in the crest exploding over the
        top of a hypothetical ocean
        of your choice, with fear, and bark, and
        possibly bovine mince.
Why did you say it that way why
did you not tell him that it was a fire in your heart, acanthus.

NEPOTISM IS FOR CAREFUL FUCKHEADS

How the dark dull hit and I
couldn't be caught in it, with a light I hit
my tail on the speed of the way out passing
this and that in a galactic swill of my mouth
wash the thing out is the process over which it passes
me my life my body my bed now rocking blanks
fireworks passing in the night over the
deleted porno hard-on replaced by the shadowy
memory of being
loved slow to remember until
the thing lights up the sky
when I turn my head the sun is just going
and the walk is a peaceful freeze
full of heart-shaped fungi
easy now to put it off that I couldn't do unless I
didn't know, later on the ideas had advanced
beyond this and that to which I turned my hand
and back again, here we are, in the cloister
choke-hold, St Augustine slips out the side
door to bury himself in the hoary bosom,
robes that pull away
speed is the opposite of the careful undressing
that poets do on their dead
heroes flesh crumbles in them
speed will melt you in the head, leave you little
time for theoretical pontification suffused prick
your eyes and hands grow lazy, full of blood
leaves turgid by means of tiny threads
a hair's breadth of water in this slippage between
the windows I'm falling fast into
a deeper safety, a comfort that holds me by the face
inserts its kiss like a match gone out

PORTRAIT OF THE SELF AS DEATH

You now have two pounds and five pence
to spend in the store. In what thoughts will you indulge
                                   they gently mock
the words. That behind them could be something inherent
other than diminutive stress? Dead again.
If they took the entire cost and split it into 150,
it would be 100 each,
                                   maybe more.
Yes, but they don't. The collective skin is
a bag of lights flashing underground.   It is
                          odd that they have outlawed
euthanasia. When really we are doing it every day, helping
each other up the steps to death. Just a few more, dear. Lean
on my arm. Dead again.
                          The swan poses up the river, a few hundred
miles from my house. Then we have a meeting place?, I intone,
Americanized. Be forced to accept the new arrivals, peer down into
their red polyester framing, their faces unwanted. Hold my heart
as a pair of hips. Rosehips though. Turn hips. Softening the rigidity
of the desk, its plastic imitated by muscle, Is that too much?, he pressed.

YOU POEM

you (walking up the road)
you, you (bird with a hole in its wing)
you you you (thought under pressure)
you you (didn't see what I was) you you you
(now see what I was) you you (a space
opening up between me and myself)
you you (a breath I took through being alone)
you you you (thought reduced to doubling) you
(blatant reformulation of) you you you (and me,
me, reformulating) you (a praxis) you (not
singing exactly) you you (can be forgiven for
everything) you (absolutely everything) you
(draw the lines according to what) you
(forgive, arrive late to the games) you
(a staging of battles) you you (just wanting more)
you you (of a nonspecific bounty) you you
(more and then less of me) you (music rising)
you you (up the stairs my thoughts climb)
you you (impose a structure onto the impossible)
you you (eternal suspension)

A HOW-TO LIST FOR GIRLS

In a melange of people who are kings
of their own capital it's important
as the rate rises clam-like, aphrodisiac, to the outcrop of cream
coming off, to say — I can't manage a global perspective.
At the fringe of roses frost thwarts itself, at
war with itself, when I say 'America,' and everyone goes off. At
the last moment I will pull back and wipe mascara from my cheek. A cold
grey dribble, a tear wearing stockings put it there, ugg
boots kick up plaster dust inhaled by Mario, who is building and François,
the butcher on his morning
roundabout the circular town, wearing an apron
and a flat slew of black
hair. Bloody yellow apron. He does not think
it healthy for a civilisation to clean itself
so irregularly. He shouts up the window at me,
you'll burn up in zat tin can zat you live in! I point back the shadows of birds
creaming off the shadow on the roof-terrace of the unit blocks.
The sun is melting my Vaseline, acrylics, mice skins and separating
the emulsion into two liquids. Sorry about the
that I am sitting in one place whilst death exacts things in other places.
Forgive my tin-can of immorality. Not even the sun is touching me,
how can I expect you to supplicate reason. He suggested his girth was wasted
on a person with a problem like hers. I had better wipe the crumbs off the
counter-top,
appease growing wrath, buy the right shoes. And the job interview still
nebulously
unfixed. I avoid shopping at all costs this morning, and
as a reward, the bus is right there when I get to the stop.

SO FEW RICHARDS, SO MANY DICKS

I met my match in Repo 105.
I am not a tactical representation
fidelity freak and I won't tout any bullshit beyond
Dear Poems,

Today I love you. You are much better than Twitter can
eat itself, just ask
                    any number of Severins,
all of whom speak so slightly, rocking the
square mile between friends. Half a
billion for them
on bended knee to
            stocks & shares
of total compensation, no particular
name to epitomise the urban contagion,
any number of litigations
            await him/him/her there,
            but not really or only perhaps,
            man of the year. O heartbreak of the
such aching tenderness
that we fought for
awaiting you in the hundred dollar Florida mansion,
fangs of gold plate plumped around some
kind of sickening prick on fire at the
tennis she opens her hands to receive.
You know it's for the best.
Wilfully opening and splitting her tongue,
I, Man That Resembled Lizard
break next into your throat out
of which beckons song
to me it all resembles the past
if I look incorrectly
on time

          for the gold-dusted paper futures
contract traded inside. Caught a
child and held rocked a
circle in the mirror tipping outward.
Let's make our own fucking money.
Kiss up to dick
-in-hand rhetoric.
You be the bar.
I'll be the drinks, in love with
every motion of the face
revealing its characters,
Father, Goon, and Executive Fucker
all dance ahead of the bus and in between bad practice
yogic breaths sever them from the Robin Hood
Foundation sucking
out the compensation of love stocks
and shares awaiting you and Bob as well,
whose atom was split by Sumitomo Mitsui in the early 2000s.

Not merely was I a political
   secretary but possessed
of the ability to withstand the most egregious battering
   of capital organs about my own head
and in that various head cracked truth,
   that vaporous sheen meaning nothing collectively
but which upset the clockwork of days with
   anticlockwise vibration, every day.

A financial time of the lyric
   self, look oh, how you shined salmon pink
if not out, then inside, and fell at
   every opportunity, oh, just
nominate Cassandra's hit single of death.

We are all each one of her
clearly visible to ourselves and even
    then only at cost and regularly
preferring not to know.

Pleasure you with a rolled
    -up *TLS*. Everyone will be happy

not in denial of shit but in accordance with it.

Shit is the happening standard
visible almost exclusively from the inside
and we almost certainly we cannot deny shit, and
so why would we deny shit
if not to thank shit for promoting awareness
about the proximity of shit to our live
breathing, in and out in time to distance
on time for the rendezvous organised in
accordance with the boundaries shit delineated
when controlling my means of production means
I got my pen
I got my pen I got my pen
my pen my pen my fucking pen
I got my pen I got my pen I got my pen I got my pen
and with it pen
what could be termed variously a shit
lyric a sad
posture a broken vision a pleasant
bath time.

Your girlfriend is
    a fox. She
She fucks foxgloves
    to death and song penetrates

the window, some passing offshoot
  of spring and the earth on fire.
Each winter longer than the last and this one
  becoming with free and fair
reckoning unbecoming
  maybe tax you more, maybe not
who can say.

This season I will mostly be
  into owls and stocks
and butterflies and intrinsic value
  and glycoprotein.

Whoever you are on a given day moves
towards my retreating back. Love you cry and bake up
the cookies and then eat them up. Someone will whip
up the back of your neck, egg whites whispering
there that there will be a grand future
s contract, promising to alleviate our long history
of debt, working for free as we do for the sake
of being better and more inspiring and fun than
for example the TLS. But fuck
ing who works for free Dick
Fuld and the Dead-Beats,
Ozz Spazz and the Meat-Heads,
Tyson Sparrow and the Jackrabbit
of Death do not work for free speak
into my sleep with the silence of nothing while
drugs grip your wife, stressed out and toxic with
every Chinese minute planned right down to the
last blow dry planned months in advance by Chris whose
own planned blow dry creates passionate planned waxed
sex whose widower plans to pay off the credit card bill,
                              but with love.

We could be and will get poorer
  as some richness takes over or we will
get richer as some poverty takes over in a
  bitch t-shirt, cope with me, leman,
attend to me, attend to your
  brother, leman, but so many brothers
now are staking you out
  for the count says I can trade
this air too and float
  my fucking stock out with wash-pegs.

There was a crash but nothing ever ended.
  The abused become the abusers
sometimes in the amorous method.
  Care does not omit the newspaper,
the blank pathos of infatuation
  the knowing the world, the making it better,
that better is a bind, and loving you,
  and wanting more for you, all bound.
So many of you, so many of me
  all wanting all relative all.

Strategically placed rubble, triumvirate of sneakers pipe up. One two three,
go symmetry a single laughing fist in the air. Over the clipped heads of still riot
gear pops a digital camera kid prop, and the other guy grinning in
large boots. See
how I am a character
of myself of which I play and shunning all accusations of such, oh
give me a bracket! We cue him to start running.
I roll with the first
of May punches, an anniversary is a call to riot
these days is rebellious kids making gleeful moan amidst windows where
smashed and some
shops were sort of looted, where
cameras hide out in the jewellery shops. Before, that
damage meant murder so if you were looted it was because they hated you not
because they hated who you worked for. Hey but that's the same thing.
Ok but not seriously,
look, they're grinning
on the Strässe wearing orange war pants and
running about. Cannon
shot water barrel of rubber, those kinds of things but meanwhile
elsewhere worse things happen just not in the name of capitalism.
Hoodies mimicking threat
I like those. No
I don't I am indifferent, I am paper, news
paper. Jeff says, let's put an Evian bottle
at the fringe of white mist. Implicate it,
maybe it belonged to one of the 'rebel' characters. Mock their joyful rage
I reply except the thing is that you can't really mock joyful people as
they are incapable of discerning your intent, and you
are the one who ends up mocked, in a sour mirror so you
set down the bottle, knowing that modernity will speak for itself.

THOR

THOR

THOR

cut like a horse

       tell me again
how you blew
       the hardy boy

POEM

Now I just feel
older and to fail he
strumpet tamped
down the moral hay
fretful contingency of
we roll again against press mine to the wall
where it's cold and I want
there to be nothing there unheard
simpering
and ready by turns to invade
the legs
it will not be most of an immediate category
cavity
she stretches tailored and up-done
well the weather hangs away from us
the meeting's horizon glitters
like a trail of dolphin snot
he has ruined the song for me
but also brought out its repetitions
made clear how it mourns

Scarlett tweets woefully from the airport. Flight delayed.
She is maybe genuinely disappointed in a lax-
ative commercial
it's a very romantic setting,
air spliced with
moan tones
for download in the bath
you'd never do something like that, only in a mimicry
of your own inflated head, you,
you there
blow them to the digits there
LO, SHE BLOWS
SHE BLOWS THEM TO THE DIGITS THERE
blusters and blathers
and mimics and slavers
and you love her
rancid soup alloyed to the pink inflating V
that rises above the spraypainted tinkle to make
me cry without moving my new face. 202-224-3121
to call your representative from the tub. Rinse and
magnify thy holy mane
of yak hair. I dont now,
so don't ask me, it's rumored the boys get head
from the assorted gathered girls who do not feel safe
with a policeman in their home:
[enter scarlett]
scarlett: Time for my Xanax! =)

PORNOGRAPHICA: LITERARY OR OTHER ITEMS OF
PORNOGRAPHY

LITERARY OR OTHER snap sunset methods

It is the syntax that makes it so troubling, the thrashing

sluts, the PTSD. What are the

plots, he asks. The plots, it's all

it's all about the plots. I realize.

I buy PVC leggings.

Splayed, three paces away, a scene

that is being played out elsewhere.

Only half of the coercion is legitimate

outside of my body.

The elliptical sign. I turn away from the sign.

Deeper into my trousers.

But you can't regret history

enough.

Which images turn reason into pinkish cindered ash?
Lash trash clash crash flash rehash hash mash rashly lash trash clash.
Which images turn reason into pinkish cindered ash?
Trash lash clash flash rehash and mash trash rashly lash trash clash.
Thrash ash tie hands with flashy sash take cash and rashly flash.

The acting part is getting off cough
-cough, jerk off, doff, scoff, turn off, wave off, walk off, write off,
its only act is getting off cough-cough, jerk off, doff, scoff.

The traumas reproduce
a diffuse truce: reduce puce juice with chartreuse
misuse, the traumas reproduce   Zeus mousse
seduce Zeus, Zeus caboose.

Hurt myself herself myself himself myself yourself

trauma in the round.
Surround sound   bound mound
             surround bound mound and pound
trauma in the round.

Memory's path is deeply set,
hard to set it rightly aft.
Daft craft   buttshaft   set it rightly aft
William Howard Taft   shaft   banker's draft.

Putting power in strange hands.
Ban brand   manhandled land offhand remand.

Withstand tanned hand   planned promised land   hired hand.
No to putting power in strange hands.
Withstand   withstand   misunderstand command   demand grand land
demand grand land   misunderstand command   demand grand land.

Pretend you were one of these, lasting from the heart
on a night curled up like this in an attic belled by
lumps of light. Remove the weighted shift with
blackened tips that beat like horses' wings. A
thing can be nothing, when viewed from
above, histories, speed, and wind,
a blast of air lifting all your hair
up from the back
of your neck,

> an air of no temperance.
> Ethereal Weirdness, the
> sign reads with an arrow
> pointing to go on the
> back of your neck.

That dream of lights went out,
lights that sung, lights that blew,
light that faltered at the merest hint
of a light that was difficult, loose
in flight or tightening up for hunt.
That talked, like tape. That tired you out,
the alabaster, alabaster thing that crept.
The lie that lay and grew like a lily, like a mile.

You wait. The moment that no one else wants,
can bear to wait to hold or endure will eventually
have been yours. Stills of collisions etched into
vocal chords. You pass through, are unlike
the imagined angels who won't be
able to come, at least not on time.

You have just got to keep go-
ing until you're so far down the
road you can't go back. So
easy, like cells in a frame.

The writhing descent of caterpillars. The drama with
each new day unfolding, the information arbitrarily
coming, the air of things that had already happened,
you couldn't do it. The writhing caterpillars' descent
is a pretended dramatic moment, as if the binning of
the chrysalis and all pupations within were redolent
of some metamorphosis you yourself had completed.

Here, in the depths of my silence, I proclaim thee.
Thou art saturated vegetation, and a blue sky
tinted with pulmonary ghosts. Thou art
etc. Roped into the chair with invisible sea gear,
unable to move I fight out the long night, my
arrogance disguised as disaffection, licking the
floor as if I was writing my masterpiece
hungry for things that change no

       wait matter where you go you will encounter
these emotions, in the struggle to adapt to things
that do not quite fit, they emerge. The quaintest
dreams, associations fits of love. Back into reprieve,
dancing the same way every Friday night after night,
looking at age from the safety of relativism. The ether
burns, charged to its gable, the synthetic fabric on fire
in the sun. The thought of going back to that
stew of mid-tones fills
me with faces, each in caricature with the
help of the press. Back to nothing, no
one reside in this
sickness forever.

      Fuck you and your
vacation. For making it the best part.

                  What
do I have to do to make you understand how hard
and completely in love with you I fell that first day,
Myrtle. You were working in the garden and you had not yet
had the seven children. You were ruddy with the permanent
blush. I tore into the kitchen one afternoon as you were
baking and made love to you in the pie. When you told me you
loved me, your mouth moved like a god. Then we were
married. Not a day goes by that I don't wish I had bought a
computer back then so that I could have blogged to the world

about your loveliness. But I was just a simple farmer.
You are at my door, a gentle soul, in whose presence I remain
what I am when I am alone.

                    That door to myself now open,
I insult you with the dance cards of other women.
In your image I am dancing, dressing up at home,
economics totally irrelevant now that I am sitting
here in comfort, which is preferable to reality,
the silent echo of a metal enclosure.
                    My body surrounded by wasps,
bubbles of honey on nylon strings.
                              I took my camera that night and we made
                                    different faces into it.
                              On the horizon,
two gods worship at each other's feet. I have collapsed
into this promise of loose politics. Because I love you.
Nothing will hurt you, that's how the state would go
if it had a mouth instead of a stage manager.
Ka-boom, I lie in the bed
early, sleeping late, tugging
to get at your memory, into the
dreams in
        which you appear supplicant,
your beauty adorning
        photographs of how things were
when you were driven. Beg to be driven,
beg to be driven onwards. The air eats up my
moisturizer. Breathalyzer. See what we've done.
Deep in the soul, little tiny daisies dot the terrain.

In the end they hire the nobility to write it up as history.

YOUR EYES ARE SORT OF PRETTY

'We are not greedy,' I said to the man in Oxford Circus
who touted the Bible as his excuse, 'what's your excuse?'
I asked him, knowing full well that it was the Bible. Past clutchers of
'*objets*' in plastic, sonorous corpses fill out market research
past the jaw of heads doing what they're made for. Past
promises made by eye contact in the Tate Modern, there's little
fashion in driving an outlandish getup straight into its twin.
Why confuse us with difference, you don't need other nation-states
bringing you down, especially not Europe, the grand anomaly
full of its laws and ways. Full of 'art' and women in cages, fuck that.
What's pleasure but open doors and Greece before the flood,

rape and extended travel, and they were building buildings
tall as the hand could reach standing on the shoulders of your
lover and his lover who was also related to him, the sun making peach
and pink of everything, and children. The bullfrogs made complaint
in trees observing our habits, except by then, in Europe,
they had cut down the trees, and nothing
for it but to make paper bags to be recycled to make other paper bags

destined to contain 'the sanctity of life in all its forms', getting into
scrapes like birth, getting into scrapes like debt. Pregnancy
chip in the debit card, wet with bloody murk and everyone cooing.
Nobody had dreamed such possibilities, except me hence the shield
I come bearing arms but not to use, they're only for show, they're an
escapist's favourite dream, that's why we open ourselves at the sight of
sun.
                                    We talk about what
                              to do with waste, but
not how to avoid waste in the first place, would miss choices,
magnetic pull of red and white and s a l e or
n e w s, all of which keeps us in songs and permanence, stapled
                                    to a degree of knowledge
                        to the sofa. How much is enough
if truly stopping appeals, or blow cash like bits of glass, shrapnel in the screen
changing numbers. One bomb to remove that negative sign and forget about it.

Information now travels at the speed of light where once word
of mouth waded the ocean like hearsay. The little mammal rearranges himself
to watch and listen, to enjoy the work. Now information travels
at the speed of death, remarking its leisurely walk down Piccadilly, staring
at the crackheads loose in Soho light. Comes the sun to breed her maggots.
Actually it is flies do the breeding and leave the eggs hard and milky
in the mouths of the dead. Odysseus' mouth so teeming. His hair looped
                                                                    through the fingers
of the captain, who sells bottles full of oil which he has made himself in the
                                                                    bathroom at work.
       While regression burns, I long solely for a cityscape, to escape through story, all
that's needed is a complicit ear one such not stapled to its machine-generated postal
delivery. Flapping like a thunderstorm over the bank statements piling up defending
against the occurrence of offspring. What a comedy of death. Laugh. Turn
what would otherwise constitute waste into a beating at his brow seeking a moment
of pleasure, really, just a moment, even in a bathroom, even at a plastered wall
painted blue with an effervescence of vomit, even against a layer of vomit itself,
                                                       as thick as tequila, everything
imported, even myself, and given leave to remain, remain sculpting relief indefinitely
with Blunkett-like precision. Severed
nation-state, for whom coercion has a legal maquette working the levers
the plaintiff bowing to justice which sometimes is merely turning a blind eye or
if paying cash.
                                    I beg you Nicholas Serota
please not to keep me here any longer. Please to not allow me to loom any further
dramas, any more ontology, any more *pantomime*, viz.: Blair! SHUT UP, GO AWAY!
It is giving me character. It is giving me identity. It is giving me community.
It is giving me a rash. It is giving me the excuse I need to spend the weekend in bed.
It is giving me a transfer from the company payroll. It is my head
plugged into the socket. It is my child plugged into my breast.
It is my gender plugged into my heart,
        behind which leaps a fire behind which
        leaps its tongue of loss, its flap of need
        which I have no qualms about raising, why should I.

Sitting "at" work with skirt
wound up under the desk my thighs   pushing
fingers around an extremely clothes discomfort oppressive morning
except only in the office, and now it's the afternoon
and outside in the partly cloudy outside is a wave
                   that elicits knowledge
          that if everyone involved is
a careerist then
there is no exception, that being a rule
not in this office
or yes perhaps in this office
but above, in the lofty shade in suche ordre as they stande in the boke
of order: lawyer, joiner, idiot.
            Now the results sleep like babes in their tables, we believe
in a clean
win we believe
not that we'd have better
but that the interminable rut shall terminate

POEM

what makes me rage is when someone else's experience touches on
an experience similar to one I almost had
what I mean is it diagnoses me with the inability to achieve present tense
except like now, when I am alone and the thoughts shut themselves up

I just want you to know—
antinomian robots scaled the velvet wall this afternoon
around 4.
                        They wielded diaphanous weapons.
They went down and out,
in fiery green coats and in laser-coloured orders.
They traversed the land from the café to the charity shop,
opened and shut their brass mouths in unison,
synced tin lips to bargains,
admired the mayor's tinted megaphone
(actually a bayonet), all
in time to meet Norman for lunch.
                    Going mental I *do* do coffee I do *do* café
smash the daily heart that fastens up the petals I do
a someone, bear, a bunny, do *do* a lovable urchin,
do get paid and am slurping cement
but the someone in me comes and does
do the perfume and the kneeling does
do the coming and the reckoning does
do the sitting and the thinking,
does the elderly doing fusses the
latch for the elderly
stains in the permanent dress
yellow, obvious brown
eldership sailing
down into averages
thumbs take hold.

Just want you to know
how we go
and then come
around to ideas of ourselves,
a dog, a cat, and a fox pet you

                    as the cage of chests lifts
               and we say this of what we know:
that no moribund ovum will wretch and sloth
its gradient muck between our teeth
and no muck that does accumulate
will be tolerated if sniffed out. We,
soiled and reposed in the garden,
will take yes more and less of a beating.

IT will remain couched, equally reposed
     in the backs of our minds, its blood race the circuit
IT will not sink into disappearing
IT   eggs, modulated offerings, investment funds, lies,
IT will not collapse into romantic ideas of itself
     as collusive healing or an orgasm
IT will inflate kindness
                    will inflate the degrees
to which questionings are satisfactory IT
                         will sit up pushing its lungs out and talk about
                              inconsequential things
no IT will always repose
in reasons for gratitude
               painful word
which steeps our modalities in fire
                    the body parts
jointed, blood coursing through
 customary routes.

Be thankful that if in the armchair
it will not be the time to invite death to breakfast
          eyes pat their balls
flaps of cool thought
 bones curve accommodatingly upwards
          and no one is there
    and it doesn't matter.

Help me turn over my leaves
in your hand closely exhibits wealth
no excuse to absent bravery
to limp through guilty
muck and accolade
            how can I say this, if I want you to know
how thoroughly antinomian robots scaled the wall
this afternoon, around 4, you could conceive in it
that reluctance   that this
is as far as I will go
 for now
human dust
            lest it cracks into something like impatient love,
 the promise to give away all solid balloons,
keep affections as poison enough to be antidote,
lose the robots with strangulations of silk
                                    that posset and liquefy
                            their hard places that pet dry
                            foxes atop kitchen counters.

I want you to know me to know me
unknown and
splattered against the velvet wall, where care shines forth
where cities can be exited in a pale ruddy march
dismissing the obvious affirmations of type
running down the air into lavender valleys of sky
over which the white moon makes light of the
pink against descending blue, as real
as the inability to diversify the European energy market—
and our bones will not glow or be even remotely fantastic
our superheroic qualities will remain intangible
bone will simply be one
of many felt layers beneath skin
tissue and muscle and organ and fighting

will accord to the bravest breast
in the opportune moments
in the striations sought for within the means of Love
the means of puffed ribs
  sit forward
         move into presentment
                   presentiment
be daring with your chest
thumping beneath it no
  tepid reaction to glowing but nodding
to being up on the scale, not a withering
congratulated brat needing the lozenge
but what will always elude the critic, who
  mistaking sex appeal
                   for nobility
         will always misdirect his jump-rope, see
                   it flap him in the face.

To salvage in memory one there are things they give to try. Two.
To the new leaves turned and the past becoming new
Mounds of earth raised up. This past a part re-doing
All wanting urging
To be less apologising less
Needing in the morning the stoning
Of angels and permissive amputation someone is drunk, drunk with the
Passion of
Lyric? Ha ha poets are never funny, only terrible.
A poet is a terrible
Man in love with the world, woman
Man in love with the world, drunk
Men in love with
A death never to blossom
Never never for the end to come. Have to wonder
What it's like, at the end, for poets, even if and still
Letting go is just realising about
Holding in
The first place. It is helpful if and when the
Parents are asleep or violent at the wheel, neglectful drunk
Or charming to strangers, overbearing, over-protective
Or generally weird in some fashion. Fashion. Fashion.
Bite your tongue down into syrup, drink it off, fuck you.
How fashion became starving, an aspect of
Desperation that was given to be called beauty.
The exercise returning in saying fuck you
To everything, silly things, even fuck you
To the road, the beguiling
Unapologetic road
A damp patch, somewhere, a man

Patched up desperate,
A man hope patching sewn. Tremulous
reminders, memory.
Hope aching premise, sleeping around,
Dusk over faults, kissing among faults, loving
Among faults darling.

Today the geese know that something is up
and all goose their necks to see what all the
fluorescent fuss of police is about
the few hundred of us walking vaguely down
the authorized streets into
unauthorized being where
rows of vans block roads, police stand linked and lean
on each other's shoulders, pushing bodies away from the edges
of harm with their hands on our bodies at the edges
of Trafalgar Square.
It is a spectacle for the tourists who love every minute of us
from their stalled buses
the hands on our bodies
want to get off.
I cannot tell you how I had to
not have the right to remain silent. Not since 1994,
and I'm leaving now through the lights
and through the leaves.

We the massive majority in our bodies are few
as am I from my seat upstairs alone being with you
being with you.
I come downstairs to get out on the street,
not to tell you I am soft
but I end in telling you I am soft through the leaves walking home
as the lights light up the yellow leaves blue
and the yellow leaves orange.

WHEN PLEASE IS SAD

Please is not sad   to say only

to hear said

by a succulent head.

I bruise my lips on   *when please is sad*

HOW I CAME ABOUT THE COAT

A long process involving an incurable STD that
disappeared, the exploration of Stratford, as on hunting for medicine
as in the forest, which is how I consider Stratford, a forest
need made itself present, and need was made present by a greater need
that's the way it always happens
but I don't mean to space a poem out in such a way, so what about the
                                                                    mirror,
well it appeared as if spatially, coming out of outer space I mean
o sea events of childhood, is it their first appearance?
But the coat, the coat,
                        it was a consolation
present to begin with, a joe's jacket for the one who doesn't
make it. Who isn't touched by the same grace. It just didn't fit in the
biography. So someone rewrote, or was it I writing backwards
it was almost a complete consolation for a moment
almost even untainted by the incurable
silly morning when I looked into her state-funded eyes
the brim up with compassionate envy inverted
envying herself in light of who I am and what I've done
it was just a GP consultation, jesus, come on. Yes and just a jacket.
In back of me dead things suck in vapours. All but me.
What is it about a clean record, it means essentially nothing
but the ability to make moral judgements, come up in your own favour,
that I have done right, all along, even the stupid things.

HOT WAKE-UP

In their bed they warble, the blossoms start to come
to have kept that private now rinse yourself out
taking in steps like gathered fabric detergent and
rinsed out. A flash of leather in the nose, imagine if
you, dried, hung, your insides out, replaced, taut,
walked hoping in the little town for bigger, wider
shucked its damnable trim
you could have done better
having not chasing, being not trying to be
              alone in the afternoon with the taste of chems.

In one way or another the pollution will be necessary,
asked him to hold her knees, knees were
lonely, didn't get much stroking, he complied
warm cups over bone cups, would borrow his healthier
blood for warmth and that's intimacy if it isn't a secret
but how do you tell it.

                        The thing passes in a wash of
light and weather. Wealth drips back out the nose,
want the soil in your esophagus so much open
those lips
                 bulb of your face, narrow
                 nightmares of inaction obsess
                 to stretch stitches of time to a single moment
                 pretending you can't handle lifting and alteration
                        pull back

succeed the
          edges of light
                   rejecting the jargon lining the bins

jargon of eggshells and chicken carcass
and wrappers, totally hold me
tapering back to the first light, to draw anew
with love and no more hunger

I'll start again in wishes, the futility of the day that begins either in a wish fulfilled in having, quickening heart rate, unstopping bottle of will to live, or a wish fulfilled in being dashed, equally wished for, which will carry body back to bed, to lie defeated on its back amidst damp sheets—but either way, wish carries the day, and does it matter whether wishing was for having or not having, if it starts in wishing then wishing has created this fabulous, awful day, day which began long ago in structure of wishing, which risk confounds all other attempts at vibrancy, and in this confounding lies the tidal threat of breakdown, small and thrifty, dormant or wakening underneath the ordinary deaths and ordinary heartaches and the worst thing that could possibly happen happening regularly—and the only answer to any question of despair is breath, and the only answer to any question of how to proceed is breath, and through all the vibrant moments and darkening moments breath is the pinpoint spot where the thoughts can be persuaded to wander off. An insect dies in the hot shower stream, wings scalded and tracheal system flooded, bodies are struggling in the persistent potential of pointless agony, and coming back always to this, it does not have anything to do with anything

COCTEAU TURQUOISE TURNING

COCTEAU

The like of this imbued with symbolism's
like he spoke the end to the beginning. Grind
stole her from me, rinsed the lake out of her,
if we had stayed home, shudder, solens, prick
to reverb saddle leather of solemn journeys,
turpentine eyes become altered that clasp of a
moment with her, viewed, put me to her aspen
breast hereditary pressed poison. Memory let's
that out. In moving houses we create, with
vast and final need, abnormalities and he went
on distractions, wide as the eyes is pins. Kohl
veer over brimmed lash you want to kick up
the flick you took her from me, stodgy spirit
waited pulsed anhedonic in legless, rode under
me waiting, stood you down into me as a boat
knows water to best next occurrence, float. Get
off on awaiting the silkworms of memory, their
olive shells and crass clattering comforting
texture as painful her softened skin climbs
its fingers into my hands bled in softness says
Cocteau. Turquoise turning to stone under
ground, being with her some of the finest bones.

To inveigle us out of wanting to inveigle
glow veiled her partition of weekly nos she
had clouded and come over. The sky not over
cast some doubts into floss; shingles and wash
tiles; stems of dried sticklers, blackberry brush
too feigned or feint for that particular shape
of weltered her complexion to this ending,
blunt-shaped, faltered, flattened the lids
focused. Insisted, wanted, for long waits for
lorn waif in zippers and account cars so
moody to learn the best next way of hood,

as a way of brimming girl or woman, soon
be done, moon, tuber rose. Flash of glass
in his one run movie, the alternating roles,
the picture moving to glassy smoke, sky
base on fire at horizon's curled tip. He is
in colours a trigger, worse than Adam, we
slowed up at the dusk riot he said loaning
you this hat, swatch of calcined brides
making clack on those guns pivoting not
machines forces of vision, tensions in that rot
gut of tender love. Which she drank up.

The weather in here is warm dark, incurs
wrath punishment wreathes or writhing in
stone around her wrist, appendage. Go full
load of baloney he spoke again. The lone
trap a dark set of jewellery, and him the
bracelet green plastic. Eyes wilting aided
by turtle green spinach eyes stems broke.
Shut off, shut out of the true tale only he
could speak as only he could speak, nuts
bolted to lips of crass encouraged teeth,
teething string quivering across a set of
cheap harps. Implosion of night's riot, a
stem placed in the urethra upside down a
stamen in both places, bonkers on her the
balcony edges his teeth and soles into wine
wheedling and dripping from the sphere.
Flesh sphere, to cry from, nibbled and
dripped calcium here and just everywhere
you find me when looking in dust, then
I recreate he said the same moment that
vibration barely held taut, good music for
my love who I walk the world to engulf,

TURQUOISE

not knowing anything or her name. Rich
susurration of words at soil's thumby reach
and he gluey gibbers, love is here love has
still remained and nothing is mine alone.
Walks that brief mountain repeatedly, up
in four and down in seven repeatedly, God
ot's black mirage its culmination never to
culminate. Marriage shaped in the clouds
they appear white they bristle and pull off
themselves, in the sky live happy people,
thrashed in our image he bolsters thrashed
into this man's image, border crossing the
goo grabs at his shoes to threaten with murk
the entrust feverish body and sickness made
big with lacking swollen bones of starvation,
could have said the growth too late the growth
embittered in one soapy blast, hair included.
Awkward faces corral each other someone's
got to, blemish on the magic we try to tell
ourselves lies in glossy red finished box, as in
death so it goes in the life as well. Stuck to a
different sort of sticking place courage depends.

The she rinsed out of her she conjured, gated,
drew back the remains of the gathered curtain
hated in gold safeness, of infants, she dreamed
and grew upon wider and wider, to a gleaming
ball of orb-like beauty, the kind that generates
in self-reflection torrid and unuseful. Witty
wanderer a correctional medicine of tools and
chopped wood he might one day find for her
a partner, to kill by, the franked remains of her
first ghost, still alive and thriving in the rose
carriage of bones. Carries her in wisps of hits

of the mock cloth, to protect and to hiding bury
the enormous growing vat of loveliness to
scratch loneliness into its weaving heart, pink
and white and creaming to do for itself what
audiences do to lights the fleeting vital fled
comparisons that cut off from life. This state
unable to generate until the word fate to his
spirit placate used Cocteau. Blinded Cocteau
with the flash and generous spit of a needful
heart, torn in with scraps to be used in the end,
omissions, collisions, the greatness of plum sky

ignites. Collision me she pleads and beckons
unbeknownst to beckoning and ripped him
away from her heart, where underneath the
flesh removed in ripping ranged a vivid image
eyes like dark twins pooling into the fatness
of their sad seclusion. And that was Cocteau
widened with intensity staring up from wounds
self-inflict her rose upon the downs of trolling
quickened ease, the quest frenetic merciless,
their four eyes rolling in steaming studded
hiss of limbs seeking slake, do you know
me would you care to know me would I whether
care Turquoise considered without time enough
to know a self in lashings or stitches knowings
set out and unencumbered, to brown butter she
thought with eyes I am so controlled afraid I
gazed into the nervous camera shook me curls
up and curled down around a snake's teeth are
squarely mine, my father's form a lash of size
no mal to overcome, no man, unless the size
of moons and eyes of mine. The ones I know do
not venture into dialogue she to the mirror said.

TURNING

Sought coal and fish netting for enticing sought
bulbs in dressing rooms and fur, which spread
out night delights to light up greasy spitting
tongues and wet stink of passion's satin, split
and frayed in nervous needs him urgently, wrest
the pallid pill from shut up cabinet, plots and
thickens her gorgeous nerve of tongue, thumb
armed with little gun the leather overtook the
washy pliable frame of fungible fabric she'd
borne in dipped in river water dregged it to the
silt bum drowned its talking virgin principle, o
no Turquoise shrieking laughed and whipped
Cocteau's promise forthcoming. That sent
the foaming spirit stealing him both and her
ruby-ness under valuation at twice the price.
That set they turned the rest to time and water
settled in their eyes that couldn't see but felt
in words the coming time of silence wrung
and coursed through balconies the separations
between banisters the gaps of ivy. Her snake
teeth pressed against the ivory teeth of him,
and throat and wasted time it caught them up.

Four mighty ones are in every pair and wearing
them thus they deceased to reduce the seduction
to living not dreaming it. He wrote to her from
across the bed loveletters Turqoise a gash of
plein lack across the sheet of what I am have been
now until your vicious heart reclaims the space
I'll face nothing but what you won't offer, told
her legs into knots of refusal she only played
at bearing a being of such weight who feathers so
they say once weighed with single fingers to get
off on awaiting the silkworms of memory, pink

and brown, to eat out their shells and crass
clatterings comforting those who had also dared
to love Cocteau, and with every scent withdrawn
into the bedchamber, of jealous or protection he
said loud as painful as her softened skin climbs
its fingers into my hands bled in softness, those
bones being some of the finest and not yet under
ground, as if they felt no other bones had clasped
the bones of Cocteau, not Mystery for example
with her delectable slicks and vanishes of looks
nor Inspiration with his wilding hands and locks.

The recklessness of order surpasses itself greatly,
in polishing motions they towards each other
made for can be nullified or as yet embraced, the
layering linked up, link them persuasions, hands,
hold them, rows, soldiers of weight and honest too
true a brew it all laughs as it all falls apart serving
all makes the glue faster. They snuck therefore as
well as turned faces away, into saints or ghosts or
the words of what like fathers saying over the
heads of books that don't get read, on purpose
or in blindness or in the weaknesses of hands. Oh
to be the boss of thee she screaming said in silence
thick and tired and strong, and offered little as a
fat fish full with rotten gills and scales, the
blue and realness of salt or sugar pounded to this
offered meat. He starved for such a plenty, owing
none to everyone, could have wished to hurt less
but instead could only say yes, and gnawed down
on the bone, which came much faster than was
sought. But that's all past. And everything is past,
in order that we might seal it with a say, in order so
when next it comes we can be less prepared and less.

Postscript

He cursed her, towed she, levelled the febrile
speed of memory's hundred nations, all of which
swagged and filching lashes on she like the
lone cane of what hidden fear coalesces with
snowy retribution or loving threatening birch
fist. Love twists that wish list to speed up
caboose, tunnel viewed horror show faster and.
Spat on her back, to rejoin the memorandum
spat on her, eau and eau, Cocteau she pours her
self along the griminess and lines of trash each
line and did she pine away in you and you and
over her airways the crackling proof of pining
love, eau and eau she breathed, liking to
underwater lover becoming tailed and mer
cantile, with fins as sex as fishing net as she
had caught him with her thighs around. But
turning Turquoise from her form, and Cocteau
turning, too, in form not visible in physical but
in his vision smacked it steeped it, he murred
demurred it over; Cocteau Turquoise turning,
flotsam in brightest blue, beaucoup, the messy
kink of seaweed's knots enough to tie one down.

Loaming in the curdling air the vast associates
meanwhile, and, are racing in their bodice, a flap
or folded four, coerced conversing like forced
season changing, buttering the autumn crisp to
murky summer in acrylics; or offering the giddy
laugh of loving spring's accomplice, pinks and
whites are ransomed for their dark and bloodish
tongues of autumn brown. These executives in

the language of unseen and haven't heard coerce
the words to lavish orders, parading prattle of
seasonal food proportioned; the calm bounty
and pressed sincere of insincere gone running to
win its race alone. With suchlike eyes they fill
their baskets up with generosity, the word alone
ballooning and creaming up to fit a heart-shaped
conscience, widening eyes of frailty seem to the
hearts of eyes like strength of compassion. File
it like nails and information away, the sticker
reading press on or case won. As paper is
gathered and marked and ordered for days on
weeks on time passing and copses to corpses
the recklessness of order surpasses itself greatly.

MELVILLE'S HAT

Beatitude thus spake
the nimrod's heart as he quit sewing and touched
himself on the breastbone. The nature of the male
effigy, he spat as he danced upon his own grace
is a newness and sturgeon-like apparition
gliding in the mood of the gloom with a parasol
twined around its
fish have no throats, but me I've got one
pursed and supple to throat out with into
the deafening night, or light
of the kitchen table whilst ma smokes a cigarette
I get into the bath I am young
so when they make a suggestion I just laugh

ODE TO LOVE XIX: YOU RACIST, HOMOPHOBIC BITCH

I walk home with this paranoia mounting, the shopping bags
squeezing the blood from the surface of my arm that I carry the yellow split-
peas on, mouth
open to breathe or to think more clearly about letting something in,
make it brief and screw your face up and access the little gate. Show
your teeth riding the floor. Here is a place to say
as much as all is rabid: tenderness. Push him to the floor and hold his face. The
reality is
not so good but
putting breath into someone else's mouth is
one way of spending your Sunday night, 21:17-33, but keep it brief. It has
been nothing more than brief now for many weeks. Aving it large is
going down the pub, we do and then
back on the floor,
beneath the half-empty Asahi bottle and the garbage I compose
a letter to Orange Broadband, refuting their lies and my landlord
runs liver-coloured through my head, grasping individual. Set into me,
diamond-quality latex. I punch the ravenous slap in me that drags on
and on in company against innocent people. The need to shout gets hard
to snap but I'm tired of monitoring my karma. The cynics insist that it does

                not exist,

mostly because it is such a gay word. Permission: OED. The spine curved
against his thighs. The state of being. The state of
Texas.

  Some fanatics in the state of New York are thinking of banning the
"n-word" from popular music, at last seeking where they cannot recuper-
ate to eliminate. This is society's answer to dialectics. Total language ban,
then what happens do you get imprisoned? The freedom to repeat the
word within a community context appropriated by those whose ancestors
suffered under it is a motion towards renovating its history. Leroy Comrie
says the meaning of the word cannot be changed. Has he lost his OED?
In Venezuela when they say *chévere* they do not mean *cheg ebere*.

     Look, I really don't know how I feel about this.

      Political correctness is wrong because

how is it political? But I won't say so. Stop being so white. I feel as though I

should. I feel

as though I should but not today. I feel as
though I will. I feel as though I will but not today.
Without permission I am just narratives inside,
each flying into the window-glass, knowing it is the sun.
Without permission I am the bugs
desiccating in the bulb. Without permission I am accumulating
funds and then spending them how dull
it all is but for love. And then
back on the floor,
I love thee depely. Break a
line. To do lines of you
permanently without letting go or it
getting light out or something bad creeping in, so much love
stating the limitations which are just
going to break and you flood past them, very far, Domingo F. Sarmiento.
I love thee helplessly, so much the end of life appears. Both
thee and me are in thee now, which is why I know
thou wilt go to the defendant, Symine Salimpour,
and lock her mouth up with Hollywood money,
the perfume *Shiloh* evaporating. The soule is then taken wyth covetynge.
I'm ready. Through careful definition. Some
minor doors are shut perhaps but all the rest are open.

FIVE HELD IN MARY-ANN MURDER

Today speculation merrily careens
over the grassy murders carried through the press
in five versions variant
on definitions of harrowing
hope/expect
the worst, and in the papery gloom
of a low afternoon I shun the negatives
whilst trousers protect from simpering
stares my body
mashed to its seat. RSI begins its journey down the arm,
wondering about the nature of
how twee is the movie version
of us, out of the guesthouse where 'ordeal' is spelled out on inflated
bloody paper balloons, stretched across the walls of bliss or blue lace
rhododendron or the remote desert island
              into which you make eyes
      switch off   it says
into the ear and whispered, to respond as I am
to respond, does beauty affect
torture, and
or inflict it

YOU PUT THE FIANCÉ IN FINANCIER

Come on don't leave me just yet, if I haven't figured it out. Come back for one more kiss that will turn into fruit trees. Not to wish for the metaphor overmuch. But at night when the tunnels are coaxing with curled fingers slogans in colours and wishing and I've looked up at the sky only to find it filled with Canary Wharf, the red dashes of light comforting as the night closes in, and would like to bed down in there under the desk with you, in our blanket of wasted 30gsm, and steal ruined, pasty kisses like sleep returning after too long away but the goal is not sleep or nature or money it's just making sure we never get there, then? We get paid, probably, I don't know I guess like I said it's not about the goal. And down the street you weave amongst the trees with blossoms, inviting the rain to flood your front room. The leaves trying to get in the front door, with the balance sheets thinly resting amongst the shoe trees, I guess there are things we are asked to carry in our hearts and the asking is so gently put that we do or that there is something inherently sexual about forward interest rate curves. It's your life, as you like it. It is me too that wants the key, sucker for mythology and advertising and those workdrinksjewelleryfuckers who think everything is fabulous.

CHANGE THE GAME

The young girl spreads
her eagle wings
has made men men, their chortle cheeks
of epithets. It always hurts
if when made of razors having
zip to blunt the edges with but petals,
them so obviously pink, the detail lost
to continuum. Break
break break break insufficiently break
break piqued
about the girl who makes men men, and are we
like that, our
heads churning, and how to break across the knee
all pride, all commitments never
give me or anything anything or a name.
The fire dampened with the word for wet
a jet heart to a traitor's acting, burnt to ashes
the ships of fools I am helming
blister raised across ice, blue
sunlight, pockmarked moon,
broken philosophy
& all of it powerful

no wonder he laughed, in his palace framed with fire, in his
making the general specific, in how all that is fucked rocks
the world's atoms in the girls
who make men men
this narrative also dissolving
returning, dissolving

JENNATITO.JPG

Where to begin flash flood China doll – *literally*
pink and blue and pink and blue
hovering over the production of
candy cremes in the face drastic head petitioned
quickly into full-time love affair minus dead penetration
in the speech the language holds
drops down full collusion blood
  at the awards ceremony
   (usher myself out of a gathering
  cursing all but the vapid exclusion of love
    performed on all global others
   rinsing me out perpendicular to what I need)
 this is Twenty First Century amour
a bulldog in logo-cum-tuxedo rescues the fair from her maiden
head bazooka'd by gang rape culture insidious counts to move
cash into the blanket feed, and a lexicon of drilling seeps through
  Twitter and I leave
that particular political statement lost on real politics and out on
key informations, 1) rape victims believe self to blame
2) porn star delayed in airport on way to well-deserved holiday
  sifting through my skin I find sheaves of
  what is this sick and melancholy power
   like the power to hurt in a pox protracted
visuals go damp, all you remember is the knight in shining
sports gear and the porn star whose ass he saved – not *literally* as
                              she'd been keeping that.
Love rules even
as internet pursues archive
 gropes past a tender pax
and the dialectic blooms beneath the technicolour flowers,
hideously hot, inconclusive

like it does mine even before I've performed the little death
goes behind me like a yellow brick road
path my feet
dented lapping nerve. Safety in knowing that what holds you up
isn't alive, and therefore can't leave. Only you can leave, and you will
mouthing your twist like an undisciplined lover and throw in its face
hands empty of pen, calling it husband-hungry
in tutu with dayglo.
      Come back to me now
my love you will eventually say, long after the fact. Her face will turn
and be neither woman, nor man, but lung heaving under ocean,
the muscle perfectly formed under skin when you open the door
a mechanism whose longevity nurses you at the breast,
a site of fire that moves beneath you, first rippling and
then slowing into a drill pump between canapés the suit
contains the warble of your admissions and of ordinariness
and of everything, everything that can be said about our bodies
can also be said about the soul that moves
dehydroepiandrosterone moves my bed
as modernity refuses to pass away and you are miles away
leaping about in it, clear about life, where it goes, who to talk to,
the little years pulsing with breath, fish swim in the lung
and now life with its death is a crashing presence
a subjective masterpiece
a monster whose horns and tusks toss me
on the wind that crashes into the house.

Art pulsates within me, more than an absent child
more than the fund to help babies
more than electricity. Apple+tab
darts between worlds as in rooms I haven't the patience
to walk through
and cannot give 'no' to the food, in it pours

I want to make little words in all of the windows
make nothing for too long in one place, lest the depth appeal
to the monster, slithery-tongued, e-oriented
hiding among dashes in 'Sent Items'
waiting for a lashing of tongue.
There is no surface desire, anymore, now it goes so deeply
into me that I look and it's lost
over dinner it's lost
over the weekend it's lost
and I turn to you, startled at last to meet eyes
'*to make eyes meet*' is the song that explodes
who knows how much of me sleeps, even I don't.

Everything has always been this way. There is no greater allocation of suffering, no greater allocation of injustice. The lies are not less easy to believe. The fact of this is neither comforting nor consoling; the point is not to comfort or console, but to know how to approach living in the eye of a permanent storm with as much grace and ease as can be summoned, whether in the subtle psychology of belief or in the overt psychology of struggle, when the possibilities for sadness are immense and irrefutable—sadness is irrefutable—what can be refuted is this urge to take myself seriously—

LA PARTIDA (*The Game*)

I take up begging – it's the way the music shifts, I stay up
going through jpegs. Lightning, orange of starting day, the
warmth of the heart, a sheet of muslin bells, something
lonely. It's the city that's done it to me. Purple and orange
and red. A lonely traveller. Then the lightning again. The
dawn. The overwhelming softness of something in water
colour, the wheat bells again. I sit in the silence, waiting
for the previous death to conclude.

I flowered then by
stammering something, that was always the way. The drum
sounds a little, very gently and when its insistence grows
I have the feelings between my ribs, memories, more jpegs.

My body surges with electrical heat and goosebumps, rows
and rows of wheat where our beauty is permitted to roam
more or less freely, but not to be an observer, oh please
let it not be so. I cried out that I had done what I came to do,
and the broken light fixture was a bird, up there against the
door frame, flying through a paper dimension. The closed
door and the cracks in the paint seem no obstruction. Seek
no more to make within hate, the weary may rest here now,
sentenced to much longing. I remember I was holding my
knees and leaning forward. It was unbearable. My spine
now drips with its shame, shame of love, a buckling

of everything this is for
you, again and again it will be necessary to butcher the
lining of the vena cava, scrape out the venereal
muck, release more birds, forget about politics entirely, lend
definition to the atriae, each tenderly in their turn, action is
remembered differently now. And to make more calls, well
that will be certified. The border abounds with social things,
their beckoning difficult now to understand.

HARMONY INC.

At last you're tired of wanting. You're fed up.
In ride the forms alongside the closing light
which, you appreciate, takes you to bed,
tossed leaves of sleep, and in the morning
ruin laughs and calls about the production line.
This will stick in your mind, but later.

You are continuing ever more gracefully to bear
shock. Inside of you, a woman rides to work,
her body disgusting to itself, soaked
with the sweat of commute, hair
stuck to its ears spreads a foul cloud.
Beads break up like a virus on her head.
Someone pulls mucus up into their sinuses
where it is safer. Oh fake tiger. Oh
photographs of India.

Anyone with a beard is lying. Note
that down. Make a rhythm out of some
cheaply found data which you can believe in the
same way you can believe anything else that
you are told.
          You think because it's poetry it's
funny, well it isn't, it's fucking serious.
The main issue is that you don't care anymore
whether or not you wake up.

A line of sweat runs down from the back of my thigh
to the inside of my knee, mocking lust.
Then suddenly I'm under terrific blue sky. And at the bottom
of the atmosphere and of the building I dread
the machine and pulleys that will take me up,
knowing Fergus will draw the blinds, he
knows how it upsets me but

he can't see
otherwise. Daytime dark coats the office
in its strip-lit self. The former urge to cheat now
feels laughable. Just get in line like the rest of us.

Alongside this, though, other things
to think of, both remote and imprecise,
like lunch. Sun in the grass and terrific
standards of emptiness, addiction and competition
loom, even as you crush the grass and see beneath it
slowly strength returning. Your nerve
is a magnet leading back to food items
and unbelievable references
to a strangely melting plastic mould.
'Jelly finish,' they say. Release self from suit.

                              Internet networking
is a good thing but the uptake is laughable,
I don't even know what I'm saying,
do you ever get depressed? The CEO heaves
himself to the grass, one final desperate lunge
of his stiff existence, into nature's forgiveness,
if it was any other day I wouldn't feel like this.
Any other day that's not a weekday, I mean, longing
for the salad in the fridge. But yes, he eyes
her with desire. Yes, they eat lunch together.
Yes, in the park. It was just a bit of fun. Stuff in my
pockets. But yes, the plastic mould. It sticks
to your skin, then when you pull it off it leaves
a residue. And it feels really weird but then
suddenly, a day or so later this little plastic
cervix comes out, and you put it in the bath and it
expands. Blows up. Really big. You put it
over your head. Then wait for love. Yeah it works.

Uh, yeah? You really shouldn't be so
defeatist. You believe in like literally nothing.
Please don't bring up the FDA anymore,
or Rumsfeld or aspartame or Tamiflu.

                                        Coleslaw dangles from
their mouths. The CEO hunts in his Sainsbury's
bag. You didn't set yourself a goal in time.
You scattered your resources. Diffused everthing.
Made it hard to understand how
how to proceed. Elf is your favourite polyolefins
company.

Sustained pressure of a particular frequency.
                           Monsan— Monsanto—
Monsanto, close to me.
The collapse of reason and good cheer into need,
everything cathected accordingly, with a view to
falling back in love. You buy this mould – no,
you buy this plastic mould, and let it
stick to you. The residue
forms the product. Cuntomatic.

There is such innocence at the root
of the most incisive evidence
of global intellectual decay.
                                         Look
at the happy Europeans, frolicking.
I love their smiles.
Open my coat.
Expose the heart.
Sun dries the blood.
They start to disperse. Drifting back into
rhythms and hunger. Pointless emails and *produits*.

PULMONARY CURVES THROUGH THE RAIN

A wet inhalation passes into non-smoking and shuts the windows.
That's a new political delineation. I feel terrible.
                                        Cold air descends
again and again, my tongue confounded and the same for my
core, struggling to sleep unaided with a pile of broken bones.
Melatonin and chamomile struggle with a comprehension of
self as words in their foreign space grow heavy with implication,
a thing I know I used to love and which I recognise returning
among the dampened certainties. Edifices plunge into
undress. Who can now correct these burnt rivers of impulse.
I tip beneath the rain and a ring of angels whose gazes
evade my own, the grammar in a crown of thorns.

                    Thighs move in sprays of perfume,
                    firmly across the bed a kiss you won't.

We are instructed to divide sacrifice among categories of sense.
I place it in negative capability. I see it in the house you won't
give up for love, and in fibrillated lust – lust which is
worn by Oedipus, napped into his visor.
Tucked above the ear of his baseball cap.

                            I wait two times, once for you.
The other time crosses its arms, is fully awake in the night,
and struggles against the embrace of inevitability. Its self
is a whispering thing, stretched out in a repose that suggests
the death of flight, or sculpted soaring bolted to a plinth.
Often time makes impossible certain aspects of the past and
the body is inclined to deny such abstract limitations.

Back in the room of categories, one of us states that revolt is
immediate, and breaks incontrovertible things. I say it is constant,
an attitude felt in all things, and threatening all of the time.

Everyday they barbeque. I go to their buffet if only to remain amazed
at the future I can no longer envisage, blonde angels' faces turned up at the
mother, shrill voices alarms of projection, evidence of what further need they
will become. Procreation is a last resort, with love now internalized as violence
done to the self, no farming tools to signify a goodness in our plight. Our
ethical canvas is not exactly blank, but palimpsest so scrawled into illegibility.

We are born in innocence, the nexus of our excuse. In this way the race
re-appropriates inculpability as dominance, handing down cash and ideas in
equal measure, both hands' treasure bearing equal weight. Meanwhile the
great black night is illuminated by lithium which calls everything into ease.

We may no longer permit ourselves the luxury of conciseness. The various
demands of travel prevent the accumulation of dictionaries, all that which is
plugged in derives too great a pleasure from our ease. It goes in shifts now all
closer together than before, input and output. Inbox (1): do you read Foucault
in the bath? Don't worry I haven't read him either. Stand eating at the sink.

Elsewhere the countryside brushes death against the lips of a photographer
for there is no space now unencumbered with our anthropologies, debased
or steeped in theory, terrain is nonspecific exempting what we can work
the land for, love or drinks. It is much easier to roam through the brackets
of the past, reaping the intangible things and the neverending merits of death
exacted by our increasing wants and they too roam now, fields of words
passable under our greasy fingertips, I am wearing this flower-print thing

from the thrift store. Tensions are lost, even for the ex-pats in bars straining
their intelligence through disaffection. Murdered intimacies we can gawp
at once we've paid the cinema fare. I remember the city. The gallows are
still there, roped with bloody threads of plastic, deceased shopping bags.

Me underneath their memory in the night as it kicks in, wretchedly examining
what of history cannot be read, making plans aided by electronic devices, the
concept of speech now something that is written and which only afterwards is
permitted to leave my mouth. I've prepared a statement: I've prepared several.